# How to Raise and Train a
# COCKER SPANIEL

## by EVELYN MILLER

**Photo Colour Library International**

Distributed in the U.S.A. by T.F.H. Publications, Inc., 211 West Sylvania Avenue, P.O. Box 27, Neptune City, N.J. 07753; in England by T.F.H. (Gt. Britain) Ltd., 13 Nutley Lane, Reigate, Surrey; in Canada to the book store and library trade by Clarke, Irwin & Company, Clarwin House, 791 St. Clair Avenue West, Toronto 10, Ontario; in Canada to the pet trade by Rolf C. Hagen Ltd., 3225 Sartelon Street, Montreal 382, Quebec; in Southeast Asia by Y.W. Ong, 9 Lorong 36 Geylang, Singapore 14; in Australia and the south Pacific by Pet Imports Pty. Ltd., P.O. Box 149, Brookvale 2100, N.S.W., Australia. Published by T.F.H. Publications Inc. Ltd., The British Crown Colony of Hong Kong.

The author would like to dedicate this book to Three Lions . . . their wonderful photographs would enhance the value of any book.

Photographs in cooperation with Doris Cobb of Tarheel Kennel, Far Hill, N.J. and Mrs. Margaret Ciezkowski of Uniondale, Long Island, New York.

PHOTOS BY GEORGE PICKOW FROM THREE LIONS, Inc. unless specifically credited otherwise.

# Contents

As a pet and companion, the Cocker Spaniel enjoys exceptional popularity. Devotion to home and family are chief characteristics in this role, and he is usually trustworthy. (Photo Colour Library International)

# 1. Why a Cocker Spaniel?

Of all the many hundreds of breeds and varieties of dogs, the cocker spaniel has, practically since its introduction in America, been the top favorite of the vast majority of dog lovers. The cocker spaniel is known for its friendly disposition and attractive appearance but there are still more reasons for its great popularity.

The cocker spaniel is still a hunting dog. Historically, spaniels generally are conceded to have originated in Spain, hence the name *spaniel*. In Spain, during the 16th and 17th centuries dogs were used as "couchers," assisting the hunter. A good spaniel approached the birds or wild animals from one

Cockers make excellent pets. They love children. This is one of the characteristics for which they are bred. If you have a bad tempered cocker spaniel, it would be wise not to breed her.

side, while the hunters approached from the other side. As the dog scented the animal or bird he came to something like a point and his tail wagged like a fast metronome. Seeing this signal from the dog, the hunters would quickly close in on the game, pausing before they reached it. This allowed the spaniel time to flush the quarry so the hunters could net it. (This was before guns were invented.) The smaller the spaniel the better — as it could then come closer to the game without being seen or heard.

In 1859 at a dog show for hunting dogs only in Birmingham, England, a new type of dog was entered into competition. Called a "cocker" it was entered in the spaniel class. A few years later came the first written description of cockers. "Light and active spaniel-type dogs ranging in weight from 14 to 20 pounds. They have round heads, raised foreheads, with muzzles slightly more pointed than the springer spaniels, but ears less heavy. They have a small setter-like body."

The Cocker Spaniel still ranks among the ten most popular dogs in the United States. From 1956 to 1976, more than 20,000 Cockers were registered over the '56 figure of 32,003. In 1977, this breed moved up to fourth place in popularity among pedigreed dogs registered as reflected in the American Kennel Club registration figures. That number grew by almost 7,000 between 1976 and 1977 alone, with the total number registered in 1977 being 52,955.

## HOW TO BUY YOUR COCKER PUPPY

The following set of standards is the latest adopted by the American Kennel Club.

SKULL: Well-developed and rounded with no tendency towards flatness. The forehead smooth, the eyebrows and stop clearly defined. The bony structure surrounding the socket of the eye should be well chiseled, there should be no suggestion of fullness under the eyes nor a prominence in the cheeks which like the sides of the muzzle, should present a smooth, clean-cut appearance.

MUZZLE AND TEETH: To attain a well-proportioned head (which above all should be in balance with the rest of the dog), the distance from the tip of the nose to the stop at a point on a line drawn across the top of the muzzle between the front corners of the eyes, should approximate one-half the distance from the stop at this point up over the crown to the base of the skull. The muzzle should be broad and deep, with square, even jaws. The upper lip should be of sufficient depth to cover the lower jaw, presenting a square appearance. The teeth should be sound and regular and set at right angles to their respective jaws. The relation of the upper teeth to the lower should be that of scissors, with the inner surface of the upper in contact with the outer surface of the lower when the jaws are closed. The nose of sufficient size to balance the muzzle and foreface, with well-developed nostrils, and black in color in the blacks and black and tans; in the reds, buffs, livers and parti-colors, and in the roans it may be black, liver, or brown, the darker coloring being preferable.

EYES: The eyeballs should be round and full and set in the surrounding tissue to look directly forward and give the eye a slightly almond-shaped appearance. The eye should be neither weak nor goggled. The expression should be intelligent, alert, soft and appealing. The color of the iris should be dark brown to black in the blacks, black and tans, buffs and creams, and in the darker shades of the parti-colors, and roans of the lighter shades, not lighter than hazel, the darker the better.

EARS: Lobular, set on a line no higher than the lower part of the eye, the leather fine and extending to the nostrils; well-clothed with long, silky, straight or wavy hair.

NECK AND SHOULDERS: The neck sufficiently long to allow the nose to reach the ground easily, muscular and free from pendulous "throatiness." It should rise strongly from the shoulders and arch slightly as it tapers to join the head. The shoulders deep, clean-cut and sloping without protrusion and so set that the upper points of the withers are at an angle which permits a wide spring of rib.

BODY: Its height at the withers should be approximately 2 inches longer than the length from the withers to the set-on of tail. The chest deep, its lowest point no higher than the elbows, its front sufficiently wide for adequate heart and lung space, yet not so wide as to interfere with the straight forward movement of the forelegs. Ribs deep and well sprung throughout. Body short in the couplings and flank, with its depth at the flank somewhat less than at the last rib. Back strong and sloping evenly and slightly downward from the withers to the set-on of tail. Hips wide with quarters well-rounded and muscular. The body should appear short, compact, and firmly knit together, giving the impression of strength.

TAIL: Docked, set on and carried on a line with the topline of the back or slightly higher; never straight up like a terrier and never so low as to indicate timidity. When the dog is in motion the tail action should be merry.

LEGS AND FEET: Forelegs straight, strongly boned, and muscular and set close to the body well under the scapulae. The elbows well let down when viewed from the side with the forelegs vertical, directly below the highest point of shoulder blade. The pasterns short and strong. The hind legs strongly-boned and muscled, with well-turned stifles and powerful, clearly defined thighs. The stifle joint is strong and there is no slippage of it in motion or when standing. The hocks strong, well let down, and parallel when in motion and at rest. Feet compact, not spreading, round and firm, with deep, strong, horny pads and hair between the toes; they should neither turn in nor out. Dewclaws on hind legs and forelegs may be removed.

COAT: Silky, flat or slightly wavy, soft and dense; excessive or curly or cottony textured coat is to be penalized. The ears, chest, abdomen and legs are well feathered, but not so excessively as to hide the Cocker's true lines and movement or affect his appearance and function as a sporting dog. On the head, it is short and fine, on the body, medium length with enough undercoating to give protection.

COLORS AND MARKINGS: Blacks should be jet black; shadings of brown or liver in the sheen of the coat is not desirable. A small amount of white on the chest and throat is to be penalized, and white in any other location shall disqualify.

Any solid color other than black shall be a uniform shade. Lighter coloring of the feathering is permissible. A small amount of white on the chest and throat is to be penalized, and white in any other location shall disqualify.

Blacks and Tans, shown under the variety of Any Solid Color Other Than Black, have definite tan markings on a jet black body. The tan markings are distinct and plainly visible and the color of the tan may be from the lightest cream to the darkest red color. The amount of tan markings is restricted to ten (10%) per cent or less of the color of the specimen; tan markings in excess of ten (10%) per cent shall disqualify. Tan mark-

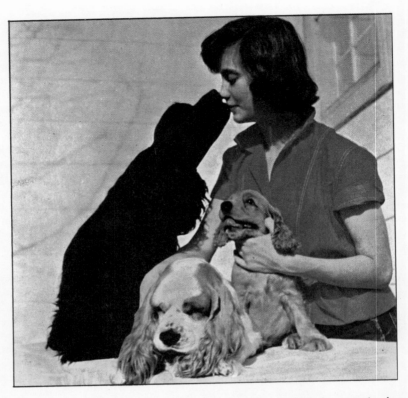

Here are three color varieties of cocker spaniel: a jet black, a parti-color and a tan. The color of a cocker has no bearing on his behavior. All cockers are lovable and intelligent.

ings which are not readily visible in the ring or the absence of tan markings in any of the specified 19 locations shall disqualify. The markings shall be located as follows:

(1) A clear spot over each eye.
(2) On the sides of the muzzle and on the cheeks.
(3) On the undersides of the ears.
(4) On all feet and legs.
(5) Under the tail.
(6) On the chest, optional, presence or absence not penalized.

Tan on the muzzle which extends upward, over and joins, shall be penalized. A small amount of white on the chest and throat is to be penalized, and white in any other location shall disqualify.

In the Parti-color variety, two or more definite colors appearing in clearly defined markings, distinctly distributed over the body, are essential. Primary color which is ninety (90 %) per cent or more shall disqualify; secondary color or colors which are

A magnificent pair of pet cocker spaniels.

limited to solely one location shall disqualify. Roans are classified as Parti-colors and may be of any of the usual roaning patterns. Tri-colors are any of the above colors combined with tan markings. It is preferable that the tan markings be located in the same pattern as for Black and Tans.

MOVEMENT: The Cocker Spaniel, though the smallest of the sporting dogs, possesses a typical sporting dog gait. Prerequisite to good movement is balance between the front and rear assemblies. He drives with his strong, powerful rear quarters and is poperly constructed in the shoulders and forelegs so that he can reach forward without constriction in a full stride to counterbalance the driving force from the rear. Above all, his gait is co-ordinated, smooth and effortless. The dog must cover ground with his action and excessive animation should never be mistaken for proper gait.

HEIGHT: The ideal height at the withers for an adult dog is 15 inches and for an adult bitch, 14 inches. Height may vary one-half inch above or below this ideal. A dog whose height exceeds 15½ inches or a bitch whose height exceeds 14½ inches shall be disqualified. An adult dog whose height is less than 14½ inches or an adult bitch whose height is less than 13½ inches shall be penalized.

Note: Height is determined by a line perpendicular to the ground from the top of the shoulder blades, the dog standing naturally with its forelegs and the lower hind legs parallel to the line of measurement.

GENERAL APPEARANCE: Smallest member of the sporting group, he has a sturdy, compact body and a cleanly chiseled and refined head, with the overall dog in complete balance and of ideal size. He stands well up at the shoulder on straight forelegs with a topline sloping slightly toward strong, muscular quarters. He is a dog capable of considerable speed, combined with great endurance. Above all, he must be free and merry, sound, well balanced throughout, and in action show a keen inclination to work; equable in temperament with no suggestion of timidity.

# 2. Bringing Your Puppy Home

When you bring your puppy home, you will need certain items to maintain him properly.

1. A harness (or collar) and lead (or leash)
2. Food
3. A suitable dog bed
4. A suitable set of feeding dishes
   (Cockers require special dishes which are designed to keep their ears out of the food)
5. Toys to teethe on and play with
6. Comb and brush
7. Suitable bathing accessories
8. Vitamin and mineral supplement

## THE HARNESS AND LEAD

A cocker puppy is as full of life and pep as any breed of dog can possibly be. As a matter of fact, that is one of the most desirable qualities of cockers. Not only is it nearly impossible to walk a cocker puppy out-of-doors without a suitable harness and lead, but it is extremely dangerous.

Harnesses are usually made of leather. The cost of the harness depends upon whether the leather is double thickness or single, and whether it is studded or not. A double leather studded harness is much more costly than a single leather, plain. For the growing puppy you can use either type to good advantage. Young puppies love to chew and if they can find nothing better, they will chew on the harness. If the harness is strong and studded, a puppy will be discouraged from chewing because of the metal and the stiffness of the leather. A good hour-long chew will ruin a single leather harness.

On the other hand, a young cocker puppy grows rather fast and in a month or two he might easily outgrow a good harness, so maybe a cheaper harness would be more practical. The decision is up to you.

A harness is placed over the shoulders of a cocker puppy. It is supposedly more humane than a collar, which goes around a puppy's neck. It is the experience of many dog lovers that a puppy is more easily trained with a collar than a harness, but you can judge that for yourself. (See chapter on training.)

A lead or leash is the piece of chain or leather that connects the cocker puppy to you. It should be 4 to 6 feet long and durable. A light chain is very satisfactory and, depending upon the quality of the chain, can either be cheap or expensive. Since the lead can be used as long as it lasts, it is definitely advisable to spend a few extra dollars and get a fine lead, one that will not break, and will be comfortable for both yourself and the cocker.

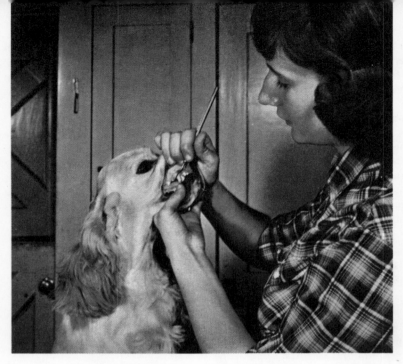

A dog's teeth are as liable to decay as your own. If you feed your cocker spaniel properly the chances are that his teeth will remain perfect for many, many years. Inspect his teeth every few weeks and if you notice any foreign particle stuck between them use a probe and remove it.

## FOOD FOR YOUR COCKER PUPPY

When you have bought your dog, the person you purchase him from should give you the diet he has been maintained on up to this time. Keep him on the same diet as long as recommended.

A puppy should be fed four times a day. In the morning give him some milk (not cold) with a little cereal or egg added (plus some vitamins and minerals). About noon feed him his heavy meal of canned dog food, table scraps, cooked horsemeat, egg biscuit or dry dog food mixed with milk, broth, or water. About five in the afternoon give him a little more milk and cereal or fine dog food or egg. Before you retire, some more milk should be offered.

Keep up this diet until the puppy is 4 or 5 months old, then gradually skip the evening milk and the morning milk. When the dog is 6 or 7 months old he can be given the heavy meal in the morning and some milk fortified with vitamins and minerals in the evening. If your puppy doesn't seem to be thriving on this diet, have your vet check him over and give you a more specific diet.

All food offered to your cocker should be clean and fresh, neither too hot nor too cold. Feed your cocker at the same time each day and remove whatever food he leaves behind. Don't allow the food to remain on the floor until he finally eats it. On the floor it gets dirty, dusty and stale, and you will soon have a sick cocker spaniel.

Once you have selected a brand of dog food stick to it. Sometimes a change in diet will give a cocker loose bowels.

The question is often asked: "Why is one dog biscuit so cheap and the other so expensive?" The answer is simple. Some dog food companies manufacture their products as by-products from other sources. For example: some manufacturers of bread, when faced with a lot of stale bread, sell it for grinding up and making into dog biscuits. On the other hand, many dog food companies go out and buy top grade wheat. They prepare their dog biscuits

Your cocker spaniel's ears are very sensitive. You must clean them regularly and inspect them as often as possible. If you discover any mites or any foul-smelling discharges, consult your veterinarian immediately. Remember that your cocker spaniel is dependent upon you to protect him against all harm.

according to a strict formula so that every time you buy their brand you get the same recipe. The latter type of dog food is naturally more expensive, but it is worth the difference because it will keep your dog healthier and happier.

Always look at the label and check the protein content of the dog food you buy. The higher the protein content in the biscuit the more food content the dog can utilize (the remainder is mainly water and indigestible roughage and ash). Thus if brand A sells for 25¢ per pound and has 25% protein, and brand B is 40¢ per pound and has 50% protein, you're getting a bargain by buying the 40¢ brand. Your cocker will have to eat twice as much of brand A to get the nutrition he needs. That's why some dogs are always eating (and having to relieve themselves). Remember: There is more waste in cheap dog food!

## A PLACE FOR YOUR COCKER PUPPY TO SLEEP

Every dog likes to have a place that means *home*. To a dog there is nothing more sacred than his own little bed. Even a cardboard box, with just a few torn newspapers will serve, as long as there is sufficient room for the puppy to stretch out. If you really want to make him feel like royalty, give your cocker a bed he will appreciate, a nice dog bed, made especially for the purpose, with sweet-smelling cedar shavings in his mattress, to keep the odor and the fleas away.

When you buy your puppy a bed make sure that it will be large enough to bed him comfortably when he is full grown. Ask your pet supplier to recommend the size best suited for your cocker.

Locate your dog's bed on the floor away from drafts. A dark corner is good enough. Many people like to put the bed behind a chair where no one will see and disturb your sleeping cocker. Placing the bed near food is not a good idea because then your Royal Cocker Highness will get into the bad habit of dragging his food into his bed to eat it. Feed him in a different room if possible.

If your cocker puppy prefers to sleep with you instead of alone, you have no one but yourself to blame. The cocker pup's first night in his new home is likely to be a memorable one for all. After spending five weeks of life with a bunch of cuddly fellow puppies and a nice warm snuggly mother, he has been cruelly taken into a foreign environment, and now he has to sleep alone and be cold! However, you must be heartless that first night. Let him howl and cry. If you have a noisy alarm clock and an old doll, place them into his bed with him and let him sleep with some company. The alarm clock will make a comforting noise and the doll will be something to snuggle with. If you break down and take him into bed with you, he will keep you awake most of the night kissing your face and your feet and you will then have started something that will be harder to correct the longer it goes on.

# 3. Caring for Your Cocker

Cockers are a lot of fun. They love to run and play. Because of their small size, they have been adopted by many apartment house dwellers as "lap dogs." In order to expend the natural energy of your very active cocker puppy you must give him something to play with. A hard rubber ball is almost an essential. He will toss it, roll it, bite it and chew it. It will amuse him for hours on end.

To exercise his teeth you should buy him a natural bone, especially treated to remove all the harmful splinters. These bones are available at your pet shop.

Toys which squeak when your dog bites into them are also amusing. Your puppy will get a peculiar look on his face when he first hears the squeak and you will have as much fun watching him as he will have playing. Crackle toys are modern improved dog toys. These heavy leather toys, shaped like bones, crackle like bones when a dog chews on them. Your cocker will love it.

## PROFESSIONAL GROOMING FOR YOUR COCKER

When your cocker puppy reaches the age of 8 months he should begin to lose his puppy coat. At the time he starts shedding, you should help him along by manual grooming.

The grooming of a cocker spaniel is not done with an electric clipping machine. True, it is much faster and easier that way, but the quality of the job is obviously inferior. (If your cocker has been ignored for some time, his coat might be so matted and tangled that it is absolutely necessary to use an electric clipper. It must be assumed that you have been combing and brushing his coat periodically, thus insuring that his coat is in proper condition for grooming.)

It is so difficult to groom a cocker properly that you must have instruction from a professional. Consult your local cocker breeder for his advice.

Because of the Cocker puppy's fun-loving nature, he will adopt other household pets for playmates. Commercial doggie toys will also help him to expend his playfulness in the right direction.

Photo Colour
Library International

**17**

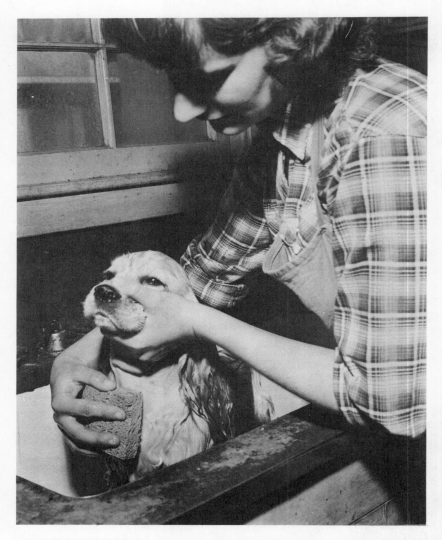

Bathing your cocker spaniel can be a simple job if you start correctly in the beginning. No dog likes to have soap or water in his eyes or nose, so hold his head firmly and watch that he doesn't accidentally get in the way of your sponge. Don't allow any water to run into his ears. Bathe your dog thoroughly two or three times a year. The rest of the time you can use a dry shampoo.

When buying a black cocker spaniel make sure his color is jet black. Black cockers which show shadings of brown or silver in the sheen of the coat or feathering are not desirable.

## BATHING AND BRUSHING YOUR COCKER

When bathing your cocker spaniel follow some sound advice. Use any one of the many dry baths available. These are merely applied to the dog's coat, rubbed in, rubbed off and patted dry. The dog is not rinsed or immersed in water in any way. Your dog will love this type of bathing and you will never have any trouble with him.

During the warm summer months you can give your pet a wet bath. Use any one of the many fine dog shampoos which are available at your pet supplier. Get a shampoo that will clean, deodorize and kill fleas all in one shot. Do not expect to buy a fine shampoo at a cheap price. You will use it only a few times a year, and it pays off in dividends if you do the job properly.

To keep your cocker looking his very best, it's wise to buy your puppy his own comb and brush. Use the brush as often as possible . . . every day if you can. It will not only give your dog a healthier coat, but it will make bathing and clipping that much easier. A cocker spaniel whose long coat is full of knots must have a clip quite close to the skin or he will not look at all the way a proper cocker should look.

Use the comb to take out knots and tangles, but be humane about it and work the knots out very slowly.

(Above) This "actor" has just been groomed. Note the full feathers and beautiful sleek appearance he makes.

Opposite:
The Cocker Spaniel was the fourth most popular dog in the United States in 1977. As a housepet, its loving nature and loyalty endears it to its family. Parti-color dogs, such as this one to be eligible for the show ring, must have two or more definite colors appearing in clearly defined markings, distinctly distributed over the entire body. If the primary color of these parti-colors occupies more than 90 per cent of the dog's body, it is grounds for disqualification. Likewise, if the secondary color is limited to only one place on the body, that also is grounds to be disqualified from judging.

It pays to groom a cocker spaniel properly and for this you should consult a professional. Here the cocker is being held in position on a special grooming table.

## VITAMINS AND MINERALS

Most cocker house pets do not get a balanced diet. Their teeth get soft, their beautiful coat gets dull and shaggy and they lack the pep and vigor that is so characteristic of the breed.

Usually this is only a run-down feeling that your pet develops because he is not getting enough sunshine, proper exercise and diet. To offset this, give your cocker spaniel a diet supplemented with vitamins and minerals. Visit your pet supplier and get some of these health preparations. There is a

Special thinning shears are used to get the hair to lie flat on a cocker's back. Note the length of the hair and the quality of the coat. Most experts agree that the cocker spaniel and the poodle are the two dogs that most require vitamins and minerals because their coats need these supplements to insure their shine, color intensity and length and texture.

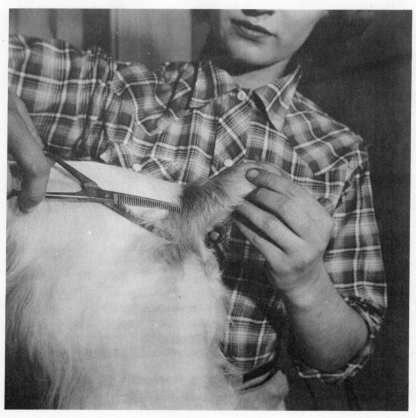

**If you have a good cocker spaniel you should breed him (or her).**

preparation (pervinal) with all the necessary vitamins and minerals in one formula. It is to be hoped that soon a manufacturer might add some of these supplements to dog food (like vitamins are added to milk).

# 4. How to Train Your Dog

## ANIMAL OR PET?

There is only a one-word difference between an *animal* and a *pet* and that word is TRAINING.

But training your dog depends upon many factors:

how intelligent you are;

how intelligent the dog is;

what your intentions are;

how much time you are willing to devote to the task.

First we consider the dog owner who is merely interested in training his dog to be a perfect home companion, a dog that he can be proud to own, a dog that won't embarrass him by untimely "accidents" nor kill himself by running into the street.

**A loving nature coupled with the good behavior you've induced from your Cocker make him the ideal pet and companion.**

## THE DOG OWNER'S PART

Before you begin training your dog to be a pet, there are certain important facts to remember:

You are a human being and do not speak the same language that a dog does. So you must try to think as a pet dog thinks; your dog will try to understand his trainer.

Training your dog is like training a child. It requires firmness tempered with kindness, strictness but gentleness, consistency, repetition and above all PATIENCE. You must have the patience to go over the training cycle time and time again until the message reaches your dog.

Did you know that a dog is the only known animal that can be bribed into learning by just a few kind words and soft pats on the back? Other animals must be bribed with food or be beaten into submission, but not your pet dog. He wants kindness and attention. Reward him with a pat on the back when he is doing well and you will soon have a dog eager to learn.

## GIVING COMMANDS

When you give commands use the shortest phrase possible and use the same word with the same meaning at all times. If you want to teach your dog to sit, then always use the word SIT. If you want your dog to lie down, then always use the word DOWN. It doesn't matter what word you use as long as your dog becomes accustomed to hearing it and acts upon it.

The trick hound dog that always sits on the command UP and stands on the command SIT was easily trained to understand the words that way. The words are merely sounds to him. He cannot understand you but he understands the tone of your voice and the inflection of the words.

Unless you are consistent in your use of commands you can never train your animal properly.

## WHAT YOU WILL TEACH YOUR DOG

Your house pet should certainly learn the rudiments necessary to good behavior. Your dog should be housebroken first of all. Then he should learn how to walk properly with a collar and leash, after which he should be taught the simple commands of HEEL, SIT, COME and STAY. Only after the dog has learned these commands is it safe to train him off the leash.

Once your dog gets into the swing of his training it is wise to continue to train him in more difficult performances. After all, the hardest part of the job is establishing a communication system so that each of you learns what to expect from the other. Once your dog learns a trick or a command he will hardly ever forget it if you repeat it every so often. Begging, giving his paw, playing dead and rolling over, are entertaining tricks which you, your friends and your dog can all enjoy to mutual benefit. There are, however, more important lessons first.

You will find that the more commands or tricks your Cocker learns, the easier it becomes to teach him more. This dog above performs one of the skills required of dogs entering the Utility Class competition in obedience trials.

## HOW TO HOUSEBREAK YOUR PUPPY

Teaching your dog to relieve himself outdoors or on paper indoors (housebreaking) is the most essential part of his early training. You must begin housebreaking while he is a puppy. Keep in mind the fact that a puppy

**Allow your cocker spaniel outside to exercise as much as possible. This will also give him the opportunity to relieve himself when necessary.**

must be fed more often than an adult dog, and consequently must relieve himself more frequently. Housebreaking is not only important from your viewpoint (keeping the house clean) but also from the dog's viewpoint, as no dog can have self-respect and the ability to be trained in other ways if he dirties his own quarters.

Dogs are a lot like some people — they will try to get away with as much as they possibly can. If you let your dog dirty your floor, then he will. If you let him know that you won't put up with this nonsense, then he will obey you. Here are some rules in housebreaking:

Take your dog outside as frequently as possible. If you don't have the time to spend with him outdoors, then obtain a tie-out picket pin from your local store and tie your dog outside until he has performed his duties. Start out as soon after meals as possible because your puppy usually will relieve himself right after he eats. Keep him outdoors until he does his duty. Once he gets used to the idea that he will be allowed indoors again as soon as his duty is completed, he will take care of the job that much sooner. That's about all there is to housebreaking your dog outdoors.

Now let's consider the situation if the weather is very bad or if you live in an apartment house and can't run down all the time to teach your puppy. It is the accepted practice to train a dog to relieve himself on paper in case of emergencies. There are also times when you are going away for the day and won't be around to take your dog out. That's where the paper comes in, too. You certainly don't want him to get sick by not moving his waste, and the poor dog won't know what to do if he's not trained to paper.

Start teaching him about paper, when your puppy is very young and can hardly walk by himself. Take your puppy to the paper every time you catch him in the act. It often helps to blot some of his liquid errors on the paper and leave that soiled paper on top of clean paper so he will get to know that this is the place for him to do his duty. It usually takes about a week.

## COLLAR AND LEASH

As soon as you purchase your dog be sure that you stop at your pet shop and pick out the type of collar and leash that best suits your purposes. Leashes are available in many different colors and materials. You can buy a chain leash, a light plastic leash for small breed dogs, or a genuine leather leash for longer, more beautiful wear.

**If you don't have a collar and lead on your cocker, make sure he stays in an enclosure too high for him to leap out of. Also train your children not to open the gate and allow their dog dangerous "freedom."**

When buying your leash and collar be prepared to order the size you need. If you don't have a tape measure to gauge the collar size of your dog, merely take a piece of string and tie it loosely around your dog's neck. Mark off the distance and take this in with you so your salesman can give you the proper size.

If you decide on a collar for a puppy, buy one that fits nicely when on the tightest hole so that as your dog grows he can grow into the collar. If your dog is older, get one with a fit that takes the collar to the center hole so that fluctuations in his coat can be compensated for with a hole on either side. Collars and harnesses are made to last a long time, so be certain that you get one that your dog will not grow out of.

Once you have the proper size collar (or harness) for your puppy let him sniff it and play with it for a minute or two to get accustomed to the smell of the material. Then gently hold the pup in your arms and slowly put the collar on him. Chances are that he won't like this strange feeling a bit, but don't give in. Just comfort him and play with him for a while and he'll forget all about it. Keep the collar on the dog at all times thereafter, except of course, when you bathe him.

## WHAT ABOUT LESSONS?

Try to make your training lessons interesting and appealing both to yourself and your dog. Short frequent lessons are of much more value than long lessons. It is much better for all concerned if you teach your dog for 10 minutes at a time, three times a day, than for 30 minutes once a day. The 10 minute session amuses both you and your dog and the attachment which develops between you during these lessons will be everlasting.

A good time to train your dog is for 10 minutes before you give him his breakfast; then he assumes that the meal is a reward for his being such a good dog. If you follow this schedule for all three meals your training program will be extremely successful.

## TRAINING YOUR DOG TO WALK PROPERLY

After your dog has been housebroken and has become accustomed to his collar or harness you must teach him to walk properly on a leash. We are assuming that you will use the collar and leash when housebreaking your puppy. Once he is thoroughly familiar with the workings of these restraining objects, you must teach him to respect the master at the other end of the leash.

You should hold the leash firmly in your right hand. The dog should walk on your left side with the leash crossing the front of your body. The reason for this will be obvious once you've actually walked your dog . . . you have more control this way.

Let your dog lead you for the first few moments so that he fully understands that freedom can be his if he goes about it properly. He knows already that when he wants to go outdoors the leash and collar are necessary, so he has respect for the leash. Now, if while walking, he starts to pull in one

**Train your cocker so that you walk him, and he doesn't walk you. There is nothing more embarrassing than to have a small dog pull an adult down the block!**

direction all you do is *stop walking*. He will walk a few steps and then find that he can't walk any further. He will then turn and look into your face. *This is the crucial point.* Just stand there for a moment and stare right back at him . . . Now walk another ten feet and stop again. Again your dog will probably walk out the leash, find he can't go any further, and turn around and look again. If he starts to pull and jerk then just stand there. After he quiets down, just bend down and comfort him as he may be frightened. Keep up this training until he learns not to outwalk you.

You must understand that most dogs like to stop and sniff around a bit until they find THE place to do their duty. Be kind enough to stop and wait when they find it necessary to pause. This is the whole story . . . it's as easy as that. A smart dog can learn to walk properly in a few days, provided you have taught him correctly from the beginning. A dog that is incorrectly trained initially may take a month to retrain, but in any event, every dog can learn to walk properly on a leash!

## TRAINING YOUR DOG TO COME TO YOU

Your dog has been named and he knows his name. After hearing his name called over and over again in your home, he finds that it pays to come when called. Why? Because you only call him when his food is ready or when you wish to play with him and pet him. Outside the house it is a different story. He would rather play by himself or with other dogs or chase a cat than play with you. So, he must be trained to come to you when he is called. Here's how to do it:

After you have trained your pet to walk properly on a leash let him walk out the entire length of the leash. Then stop and call him to you. If he just stands there looking up with those soulful eyes that made you buy him in the first place, then gently pull on the leash until he comes to your feet, even if you have to drag him over. By no means should you walk to him! If you have some "candy" for dogs, which you can get at your pet shop, give him one after you've pulled him to you. Pat his head, making a big fuss over him as though you haven't seen him for weeks!

Then walk along and try it all over again. Repeat the process until he finally gets the idea. It shouldn't take long if you are consistent about it every

**Cockers are lovable, adoring dogs. When training your cocker to come to you, all you have to do is call him and pat his back a few times. He will learn fast.**

Don't allow your cocker spaniel to jump all over you when he greets you. Break this habit by grabbing his front paws and gently stepping on his back toes. He'll soon get the idea.

time you take him out for his walk. Don't forget the dog candy because if you get him to learn that a satisfactory performance earns him a piece, the more difficult lessons will be easier to get across.

## TRAINING YOUR DOG TO STAY AT YOUR SIDE

From here on, the training gets a bit more difficult. So far the house-breaking, walking and coming when called has constituted the basic training EVERY dog must know. What follows is more difficult to teach and is harder for the dog to learn because it means he has to give up some of his freedom and playfulness.

To train your dog to stay by your side is a little harder than to train him not to pull on the leash. For the "heel training" you must get another type collar — *a choke chain collar*. It is made of polished, chrome chain and it is designed to tighten about your dog's neck if he pulls too hard. The collar is definitely not a cruel instrument (as the name might imply). Here's what you do:

Put the choke chain collar on your dog the next time you take him out. If he pulls too hard, this type collar will definitely break that habit one, two,

**While training your dog to walk by your side, you can train him either to sit as soon as you stop walking, or to stand perfectly still. If you have trained him to SIT, then have him sit when you stop walking.**

three! Once you've gotten him accustomed to the action of the choke chain collar stop the walk and start out again with the dog's nose even with your left knee. Walk quickly, repeating as you go the word HEEL over and over again. If your dog walks out past your knee, jerk him back firmly, but not *cruelly*, raising your voice HEEL at the same time. If he persists in going out in front of you all the time, stop and start all over again. Repeat this process until he learns it . . . Have patience, for once he learns to walk by your side in this manner, you will have a well-mannered dog all his life.

Some dogs are a bit lazy and will walk behind you instead of in front of you. If your dog does this, stop and call him to you and keep calling him with the word HEEL until he finally gets the idea. After each proper performance offer him some dog candy. Keep your dog informed that the word HEEL means he is to walk close to your left heel.

After your dog has learned to HEEL on a tight lead, you can use a slack leash and let him wear his normal, everyday collar. If he forgets himself, put the choke chain collar on again right away. Don't give him a chance to forget his lessons . . . and don't forget to use the same word HEEL at all times.

## TRAINING YOUR DOG TO STOP WITHOUT COMMAND

When your dog has been trained to HEEL on a loose leash, the next step in his training is to STOP without command so that if you stop for a street corner or to talk to someone along the way, your dog doesn't pull you to get going. Training to stop without command requires use of the choke chain collar for the first lessons.

Take your dog out for his usual walk, keeping him at HEEL all the time.

**After your dog has been properly educated he can be trusted to walk by himself without the use of a lead. Don't take any chances on a busy street but try him out in a park.**

Training your dog to HEEL requires a lot of patience on both your part and the dog's. It may be necessary to actually teach your dog to be patient by holding him in the desired position for a few moments.

Then stop dead in your tracks keeping the leash tight in your hands without a bit of slack. DO NOT LET HIM SIT DOWN! No command is necessary. As soon as he stops, pat him on the back and give him some dog candy. Then walk on again briskly and stop short. Keep your dog on the tight leash at all times and repeat this until he learns that he must stop dead in his tracks just as you do. When you stop, stop *deliberately* so that he can actually anticipate your stopping and be with you at all times. You can tell when he is being attentive for he will walk a few steps and then turn his head so that he can keep an eye on your face. He will actually crave to satisfy you once he has been properly taught, and he will only take a few steps before he swings his head to look at you. Next timè you see a well-trained dog walking along the street, notice how much time he spends looking at his master instead of at other things.

Once your dog has learned to stop without command and you want to walk again, you can signal him by many means. One way is to slacken your leash and then start walking so that he will learn that a slackened leash means you intend to walk again. Another way is to signal him verbally with the word "Go" or "Come on Pal" or something similar to that. It doesn't matter what word you use as long as you use the same word all the time.

## OFF-THE-LEASH TRAINING

After your dog has accomplished these lessons it is time to begin his training without a leash. Try to find a large open area which is fenced in. It will be safer to advance to this stage within the confines of that area. If no such area is available, find as quiet a street as you can (even late at night so that few automobiles are around) and begin your training there.

Let's assume that your dog heels and stops without command. After you've walked him a few feet and tested him on stopping without command, bend down and remove the leash. Start walking briskly as you did when training him to heel. Stop suddenly without command and see if he does the same. If he doesn't, then immediately snap on the leash with the choke collar and go through the training again. Walk once with the leash on and once with the leash off, until finally your dog gets the idea that he can have more freedom by behaving himself, than misbehaving. Don't forget to carry some dog candy along with you so you can reward him for a successful performance.

**While training your dog in off-the-leash work, do it in a familiar setting which has as few distracting influences as possible. The best trainer is the one most familiar with the dog.**

When training your dog to sit, use the collar (or choke chain) and leash.
Make sure that you have your dog in familiar surroundings—otherwise he
will be more interested in looking around than in paying attention to you.

It is important for you and your dog to use his regular collar during "off-training" hours, since your dog likes a recess every few days. Then when you put on the training collar he knows that something new is coming along. Every time you put on the training collar give him a piece of candy and an extra pat or two. Let him know that both of you are going to enjoy the new experience.

## TEACHING YOUR DOG TO SIT

Once your dog has mastered the art of heeling with a regular collar, put on his choke chain collar and start a new lesson.

After a brisk walk go through the previous lessons as far as the short stop, your dog will be standing watching you and waiting for the loose leash to walk on further. When you reach this point, gently push his hind quarters down with your left hand as you hold the leash tightly raised in your right hand. This will keep his head up and his butt down. Don't let him lie all the way down or cower. Use just enough pressure so he knows to sit. Once he's in the sitting position give him a piece of dog candy, a few pats on the head and start walking again.

Do this several times. He should go into the sitting position every time you want him to, provided you let him know when you want him to sit.

Remember that when you stopped your dog was standing at your side ready to go off again whenever you were ready. Now use the word SIT very often so he can accustom his ears to *that* sound. Every time you push his hindquarters down, say SIT. Keep repeating this word over and over again as you push him down. Soon he will learn when he should sit and when he should stay close to your side when you stop for a short time.

After thoroughly training your dog in sitting with a leash, go through the same method of training without a leash. A simple method is to walk along briskly, stop and tell him to SIT. As soon as he sits take the leash off and walk again. Then stop and tell him to SIT again.

If he doesn't sit upon command, hold his choke chain in your hand and force his hindquarters down into the sitting position. Do this again and again until he learns. As soon as he gets it right, give him a piece of dog candy. Repeat this training until it is thoroughly ingrained in his habits. It is always important to keep in mind that you must never start a new lesson until the old one is mastered. Inconsistency on your part is considered a weakness by your dog.

**There are many advantages to training your cocker to sit. Here we see a perfectly trained cocker spaniel visiting in a strange home. If he were not trained to sit he would be roaming all over the house, possibly making a nuisance of himself.**

While training your dog to lie down, you should emphasize hand signals as well as verbal commands. Use both types of signals during the training period.

## TRAINING YOUR DOG TO LIE DOWN

Now that your dog can sit with a leash or without a leash and is thoroughly familiar with your training routine, perhaps you want to train him to lie down. Many people feel that there is no reason for teaching him to lie down and they don't bother, but if you want him to ride safely in an automobile, training in lying down is important.

Usually DOWN is the command word for lying down although any word you use will be acceptable, provided you use the same word to have the same meaning every time you use it.

Take your dog out and go through the training sequence until you have him in a sitting position. Then walk in front of him and gently pull his two front paws forward so that he automatically falls into the lying down position. As you do this say DOWN. If he raises his hindquarters then use the command SIT and his hindquarters should drop immediately. Only constant repetition of this exercise will finally get him to lie down immediately upon command.

It is very helpful to use a hand signal along with the verbal command DOWN. The usual hand signal is to extend your left hand, with your palm down, as a sign to lie down. A very successful variation is merely to point down as you give the order. Any signal is satisfactory as long as you are consistent.

When giving the hand signal be careful that your dog doesn't think you are threatening him. You can dispel this fear by immediately offering him some dog candy each time he successfully completes the lying down maneuver.

## TEACHING YOUR DOG TO STAY

The main objective in teaching your dog to sit and lie down is to get him to stay where you want him. Many times you will restrict him to a certain room, possibly the kitchen. When the front door rings, you don't want him tracking through the house. Will you have to lock him in the kitchen before you open the front door? Do you want him to follow you all over the house whenever you move from room to room? If the answer to these questions is to be "No!," then he must be trained to stay.

Then again, what more beautiful sight is there than to see a dog "parked" outside a supermarket (while his master is buying dog candy!) waiting in a sitting or lying down position. No one but his master's command can budge him. Though strangers may pat him and entice him, nothing can make him move from the position he is in. These are some of the rewards you receive by training.

This English cocker spaniel is right at home with these children, but if strange children mishandled him he might run away from them and only the command STAY would keep him glued to the spot.

To train your dog to stay is not a difficult feat at all. Once he sits or lies upon command, proceed with the STAY command. Immediately after he is seated (or lying down) drop the leash and walk away three or four steps. Keep facing him while you are doing this, and, if he starts to rise to follow you, raise your voice and give the hand signal DOWN! If he doesn't get down immediately, walk back to him very briskly and force him down in no uncertain manner. Then try again to walk a few feet from him. Repeat this sequence until he finally stays at the command. The following day walk a little bit further; keep up this training until finally you can walk away, out of sight, and he will stay where he is, waiting for you.

When you want your dog to rise out of the position he is in, command COME (or call his name, whichever way you have decided earlier in his training). Do not allow him to run to you from the STAY position because you return to his line of vision. He must await your permission to come to you. This part of the training either makes or breaks a dog. The test is simple for an obedient, well disciplined dog. If you are lax and inconsistent in the initial stages, then it will be impossible to train him to stay.

## DISCIPLINE TRAINING FOR YOUR DOG

Up to this point you have been training your dog to act upon command. Now you will attempt to train his intelligence. This is another important part of the training problem and it is the part that separates a "smart" dog from one that doesn't "use his head."

All dogs, regardless of their training, will get the urge to run after another dog, to chase a cat, to fetch, or just to run for the sheer love of running. In the open field or park this is perfectly all right, but in the city it can be catastrophic! Let's assume that your dog has a bad habit of slipping off his collar and making a mad dash away from you. You may find this out some fine, bright morning when both of you are in fine spirits: He will spot a cat, and without warning will dash off, either pulling the leash right out of your unwary hands or slipping his head out of the collar. A moment of panic will hit you both. But, once the initial impact of the moment is over, he will come scampering back at the command COME.

*At this point do not beat your dog.* He knows he has done something wrong and he is a bit confused himself. Just pat him on the head and ignore it . . . *this time.* Then walk back to the house and get a long rope, 25 to 30 feet long. Tie this rope to his regular collar (do not use a choke chain) and also use the regular leash. Try to get your dog into the same situation as the one he bolted from. When he runs away from you again (if he does), drop the leash but hold onto the rope. When he gets far enough away give a loud holler STOP and jerk the rope at the same time. He will spin in his tracks and lay where he is, thoroughly confused and a bit scared.

Go over to him and make a big fuss over him as though you can't imagine what happened. Tell him he should never have left your side. Repeat this training four or five times and he will never bolt from you again.

You can practice the command STOP by running a few steps with him

A well-behaved dog is a wonderful companion. If you give an untrained dog too much attention he will always be jumping into someone's lap and making everyone uncomfortable.

and then shouting the command STOP as you suddenly stop short. By repeating the command STOP in every such situation it won't be too long before you can make your dog STOP on a dime!

## KEEPING YOUR DOG OFF THE FURNITURE

Your favorite sofa or chair will also be your dog's favorite seat. It is naturally used the most and so will have the odors (which only your dog can smell) of the beloved master. There are two ways of training your dog out of the habit of sitting in your chair. (You will want to break the habit because most dogs shed and their hair gets all over your clothes. Then again, he might like to curl up in your lap while you are trying to read or knit.)

The simplest way of breaking the habit is to soak a small rag with a special dog scent which is repulsive to dogs. Put the rag on the chair which

Just by looking at this cocker spaniel you can see he is not comfortable on the chair. The reason is that he was trained to stay off furniture and only under protest modeled a poorly behaved dog for this picture.

your dog favors. He will jump on the chair, get a whiff of the scent and make a detour of the chair forever more!

Another way to train is to pull him off the chair every time you catch him there and immediately command him to lie DOWN at your feet. Then give him a severe tongue lashing. After a few times he will never go to the chair again WHILE YOU ARE AROUND! The greater problem is to teach him to stay away all the time. The usual plan is to get a few inexpensive mouse traps and set them (without bait of course) with a few sheets of newspaper over them. As soon as your dog jumps onto the chair the mouse-trap goes SNAP and off the chair goes the dog. He may try it again, but then the second trap will go off, and he will have learned his lesson.

Since your dog has his own bed, train him to stay in it when you don't want him to be any place else. This can be done by saying the word BED in a loud voice and dragging him over and placing him in it. Do this a few times and he will learn where to go when you want him in bed!

## TRAINING YOUR DOG NOT TO BARK

For people who live close to another family, a barking dog is a nuisance and your dog must be trained not to bark unless he hears a very strange sound or sees a stranger on your premises. Do not forget that barking is to a dog what a voice is to a human and he expresses happiness, alarm, pain and warning in his bark. It would be impossible to write down all the different sounds that a dog can make, but you will recognize the difference between a whimper, a growl, a howl and a bark. A whimper denotes pain or discomfort. A growl denotes danger and is a warning. A howl denotes loneliness and a bark denotes strange sounds.

To break your dog of excess barking merely requires the use of a rolled newspaper. Every time he barks for some unknown reason, or barks excessively when strangers approach, swat your own hand smartly with the rolled paper, making as loud a smack as possible and at the same time command QUIET. This has never failed to stop a dog. You must repeat this every time he howls.

Certain dogs, regardless of training or breeding, howl and bark all night long and nothing short of chloroform can stop them. If you muzzle him, it

A cocker spaniel is a low dog and may not be visible to a driver. Train your cocker to fear automobiles. The best way to do this is to chase him away from every car he has contact with.

may fail to stop the howling, too. There are then only two choices open to the dog owner. Either he gives the dog to a farmer who doesn't mind the howling all night, until finally the howler grows up; or a veterinarian can "debark" the dog by removing the dog's vocal chords. Though veterinarians say this is not a cruel thing to do, it is up to the individual to make his own decision.

## TRAINING YOUR DOG NOT TO JUMP ON PEOPLE

Some dogs are so affectionate that they will jump on everybody who comes into sight in order to get their attention and affection. Only you can train your dog not to jump and it's an easy trick to learn. As he jumps up to greet *you*, merely bend your knee so he hits it with his chest and falls over. He cannot see your knee coming up as his head will be above your knee. After a few falls he will get the idea that it isn't practical to jump up to greet you or anyone.

Of course if he has learned the meaning of the command DOWN, then use that command when he jumps up. He won't like to assume the down position when he is anxious for a pat or piece of dog candy, so this will be an easy lesson for him to learn.

## TRAINING YOUR DOG TO DO TRICKS

Nearly every housedog learns a few tricks without training during the course of his puppyhood. These are usually accidentally learned, but the master observes the dog doing them and then prompts him to repeat the same thing over and over again.

You will deliberately want to train your dog to shake hands. First get him into the sitting position. Then upon the command PAW, lift his paw in your hand and shake it vigorously without knocking him off balance. Then give him a piece of dog candy. Repeat this several times a day and in a week he will all but hold out his paw when you walk in the door!

Teaching your dog to beg is done in the same manner. Place him in the sitting position with the proper command. Then lift his front paws up until he is in a begging position. Hold him that way until he finds a comfortable balance and then let him balance himself. As he gets his balance, hold a piece of dog candy right over his nose. As soon as you let go of his front paws, lower the dog candy to his mouth and let him take it from your hands. Hold the dog candy firmly so it takes a few seconds for him to pry it loose, during this time you are saying BEG, over and over. From then on, you must bribe him with dog candy until he assumes the begging position upon the command BEG. Repeat the preliminary training until he eagerly goes into the begging position to earn dog candy.

## TRAINING YOUR DOG TO RETRIEVE

Most dogs are born retrievers and their natural instinct is to chase something that moves. First go to a pet shop and pick out a rubber toy. Try a rubber ball, a rubber bone, anything that attracts your eye. They are all

The best method of training your dog not to jump on people is to bend your leg when he jumps and knock him over. He will only take this bouncing once or twice before he learns not to jump.

made of completely harmless rubber and are safe even if your dog chews them up.

Then take your dog outside and throw the toy a few feet. He will usually chase it and pick it up. If he doesn't, then you must walk him over to the toy and place it in his mouth and walk him back to your starting position with it. Repeat this operation until he learns the game. Once he goes after the toy, call him to you. If he drops it along the way merely send him back for it by pointing to the object. If necessary, walk him back to the toy, put it in his mouth and walk back with him to the original starting position. When he successfully brings back the object you can reward him with a piece of dog candy.

## ADDITIONAL TRICKS

Once you've taken all these pains to train him, don't stop here. He has been trained to learn and you will find that the more tricks he learns the easier he is to teach. Go ahead with the following tricks using similar methods of training, repetition and reward upon successful completion of each maneuver.

**A good cocker spaniel makes a good hunting dog by breeding. It is simple to train your cocker to be your hunting companion.**

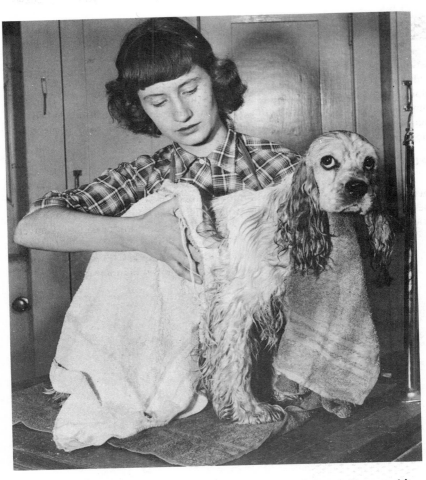

Sometimes you may have to dry your dog the "old-fashioned" way with a heavy, coarse towel. If you do this, remember that your dog must be very dry—after he has been rubbed as thoroughly as possible allow him to lie in front of the radiator to get every drop of moisture from his coat.

# 5. How to Keep Your Cocker Healthy

It's much easier to keep your dog healthy than to have to treat him for any of the ailments that can plague a dog who has been mistreated. Rather than list symptoms and cures let's discuss the various illnesses to which dogs may become victims, and try to understand how to prevent them. While we will discuss treatments, they will be for emergency use — you must always consult your veterinarian as quickly as possible if your dog becomes sick.

A dog needs little care, but that little is essential to his good health and well-being. A dog needs:

1. Proper diet at regular hours
2. Clean, adequate housing
3. Daily exercise
4. Companionship and love
5. Frequent brushing and possibly a bath now and then

If you give your dog these few essentials, chances are that he will never be a sick dog.

## EATING FOREIGN PARTICLES

Some dogs have a habit of picking up things in their mouths and tasting them for palatability. If the taste is good the dog will eat the thing, even if it happens to be a spoon with which something delicious was handled. Sooner or later your dog might eat almost anything — pieces of wood, hairpins, shoelaces or rubber balls. This does not usually mean that the dog is starving, but rather that he is bored and doesn't know what to do with himself. If *your* dog shows signs of chewing on everything in sight, give him something special to chew on, like hard dog bones (available from your butcher or from your pet shop), teething toys or an old shoe which you have boiled to rid it of possible harmful dyes or poisons.

Sometimes a dog may eat something which it cannot pass through its digestive tract. This must be removed surgically. If your dog vomits occasionally from eating some of this foreign material, then don't worry too much about it, but if he continually gags or vomits for an extended period of time, get advice from your vet. If your dog eats too much bone, he may become constipated from it and require a dog laxative from time to time.

## LOSS OF APPETITE

A dog's appetite is usually directly related to his general health. A dog will refuse to eat for many psychological reasons (new environment, loss of a close friend, a severe scolding, etc.), but most of the time loss of appetite signifies something organically wrong.

A normal, mature dog will eat only one meal a day. If your dog only nibbles on his food, when normally he would gobble it right down, you should look further for symptoms. Sometimes lack of appetite is due to insufficient exercise, or constipation. If your dog *persists* in refusing food you can be certain that something is physically wrong and a professional opinion is needed.

Do you eat when you're not hungry? Well, a dog won't. All breeders and handlers agree that it is best not to feed a dog too much food at each meal. Give him a little bit, always keeping him hungry enough to gobble anything you offer him. Though it's hard to give an exact formula for feeding quantities, you might measure the amount this way: give him only the quantity he will eat without leaving the feeding area.

NYLABONE® is a necessity that is available at your local petshop (not in supermarkets). The puppy or grown dog chews the hambone flavored nylon into a frilly dog toothbrush, massaging his gums and cleaning his teeth as he plays. Veterinarians highly recommend this product . . . but beware of cheap imitations which might splinter or break.

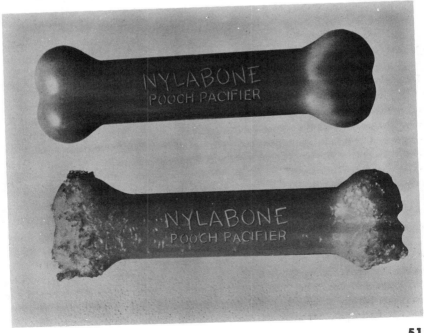

## VOMITING

Vomiting can be the result of overeating, travel sickness or bad food. It can also be the symptom of his having eaten poison, or some indigestible foreign matter. Most of the time a dog will vomit up something that doesn't agree with him. Once he gets it up, he will be fine. If, however, vomiting persists and blood or bile comes up, you must call in a vet. Sometimes milk of magnesia will be helpful in settling his stomach. Give about a teaspoonful for a small dog and twice as much for a fully-grown, mature dog.

## LOOSE BOWELS

Loose bowels, or diarrhea, is a very common ailment with most newly-acquired dogs. The change in diet, the excitement, overfeeding, all have a part in this. Diarrhea distresses not only the dog, but also his master.

The best way to stop diarrhea is with milk of bismuth, kaopectate (an apple derivative), or another similar medication sold at your pet supplier.

Sometimes a dog will have persistent diarrhea. This is a very serious symptom and you must suspect worms or even distemper. If your pet seems to have loose bowels all the time, seek advice from your veterinarian.

## CONSTIPATION

A well-balanced diet is necessary for a healthy dog. Food that is too rich or too starchy might cause a binding of the bowels. Unless your dog is properly exercised and given regular opportunity to relieve himself, he may become constipated.

Your pet supplier will have handy dog laxatives to recommend. A mild lubricant (a teaspoonful of mineral oil) will also help the situation. If relief is not forthcoming from these sources, consult your vet.

## ANUS SCRAPING

A dog has special anal glands on both sides of his rectum. These glands fill up at times and may itch and burn your dog to distraction. Usually he will try to relieve himself by dragging his rear quarters along the ground. If he can apply sufficient pressure at the correct spot the glands will empty out. If itching persists, have your veterinarian empty the glands. He can do this very easily.

Do not make the mistake that many people do. This reaction to an itchy rectum is not the result of worms! Worm medicine will not alleviate the condition.

## LICE, FLEAS AND TICKS

Dogs are sometimes afflicted with external parasites. Depending upon the intensity of the infestation, you might easily cope with the situation yourself.

First treat your dog with a suitable powder for fleas. Buy a special powder for lice and ticks at your local pet shop. The directions for its use are on the package. After a few days using the powder, change your dog's sleeping quarters. Wash the bedding material in disinfectant or throw it

If your Cocker Spaniel is a prize winning specimen, you should seriously consider breeding her to continue the excellence of the breed.

away. At the same time, bathe your dog with a strong disinfectant type, parasite-killing dog soap. There is also an excellent liquid that may be placed in the rinse water that will kill fleas, lice and ticks. If this does not rid your dog of parasites then consult your veterinarian.

External parasites are rarely dangerous in themselves, but they cause a dog such great discomfort that his entire personality is liable to change. The best insurance against this is to take immediate action when your dog starts incessant scratching.

## INTERNAL PARASITES (WORMS)

Every dog during some stage of his life will become a victim of worm parasites. These worms live inside the dog's body, usually in the intestines where they rob the dog of a great deal of its food.

It is important to know what type of worm is living in your pet as some worms must be treated differently than others. If you are fortunate enough to see the worms (or pieces of them) in the dog's stool or in his vomit, study them so you can report their size and shape to the vet or pet supplier.

A puppy might actually swell up because he is so infested with worms. Adult dogs may swell too, but more likely they will lose weight, become listless and finally, if not treated, die of malnutrition or pneumonia (because of their weakened condition). As soon as you suspect your dog has worms, "worm" him. There is a medication that you can purchase at your pet shop. The size capsule you must use depends upon the weight of the dog, so be sure to know approximately what your dog weighs. Follow carefully the instructions on the label.

## ECZEMA

Eczema is a general term applied to loss of hair or rash caused by poor diet, an allergy, an infection or poor grooming. The "dry" eczema starts with a scaly, persistent dandruff which progresses to a balding of the infected area. "Wet" or "moist" eczema is usually the result of an allergy. It itches and burns your dog to such a degree that he will scratch himself until he bleeds. If the area is within biting range he may even tear bits of flesh from the infected area, so intense is the discomfort.

Successful treatment for eczema is predicated upon finding the cause of the malady and preventing your dog from scratching and biting himself, before he causes a serious local infection. It is essential that you consult your veterinarian. Sometimes it is considered more humane to put the dog to sleep. Let your vet advise you.

## MANGE

There are two basic types of mange. Both are caused by parasites that are microorganisms. The first type, and probably the most difficult to cure, is demodectic (follicular) mange. In this ailment the parasite works its way into the skin and surrounding tissue of the hair roots. Intense burning and itching results, causing the dog to bite and scratch himself very severely.

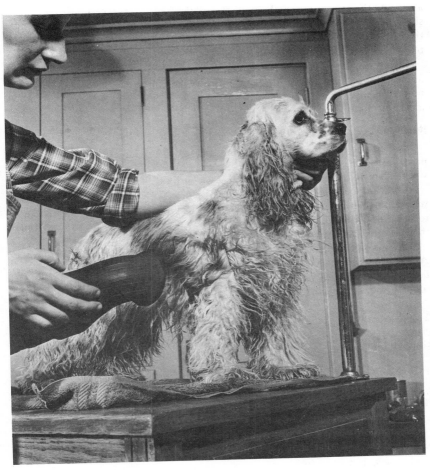

There are two ways of drying your cocker spaniel. The safest and easiest way is to remove the excess water first with a towel and then use a hot air blower. (The kind women use for their own hair works fine.) It is absolutely essential that you dry your cocker's coat thoroughly right down to the skin, as otherwise he might become chilled and catch cold.

Large hairless patches will mark the site of infection. Treatment and cure are very difficult, so consult your vet.

Sarcoptic mange is also called "scabies." It is caused by a small insect that looks like a small crab. This "crab" digs in just under the skin and makes life miserable for the unfortunate dog. Consult your vet for treatment. BOTH TYPES OF MANGE ARE COMMUNICABLE.

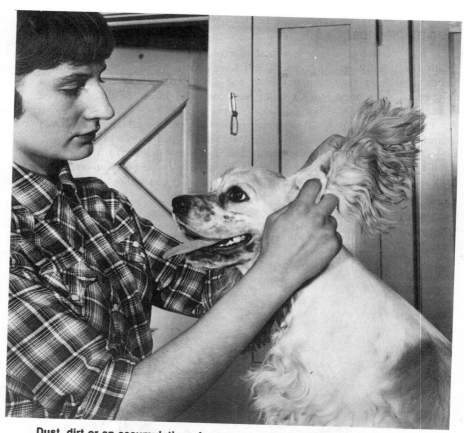

Dust, dirt or an accumulation of wax can cause an infection in dog's ears. Cleaning your Cocker Spaniel's ears regularly insures against such infection.

## EAR DISORDERS

Dogs, like humans, have ear tubes that are dead-end streets. In these tubes dust, dirt, wax, hair and mites can accumulate. If you do not clean your dog's ears regularly you can expect trouble. You can clean his ears with some mild soapy cotton. Use the end of a cloth or your finger with the cotton. DO NOT JAB THE COTTON IN WITH A SHARP INSTRUMENT.

If the ear has an odor or you see a pus-like discharge, call your vet. If you notice little mites moving around the ear tube, get your vet in right away. He will be able to prescribe an oil which smothers the mites.

Your dog's ears are as important to him as yours are to you. Take care of them for him.

## TOOTH DISORDERS

By the time your dog is a half-year old he will have lost all his baby teeth (he usually eats them) and will have grown most of his permament teeth. Assuming your dog has been fed a well-balanced diet, has had a proper teething bone, and has not been sick, his teeth should make you envious.

If your dog has bleeding gums, impacted teeth or tartar accumulated about the base of his teeth, consult your vet. He can easily correct the situation.

Tartar is a normal phenomenon, but if it is left uncleaned it can easily lead to gum infection. Make a habit of bringing your dog to your vet twice a year for teeth cleaning, nail clipping, ear cleaning and a thorough physical examination.

**The Cocker Spaniel's natural retrieving instincts and good mouth allow him to retrieve from water as easily as he does in the field. (Photo Evelyn M. Shafer)**

## DISTEMPER

Distemper to a dog is like cancer to a human being, a horrible, often fatal, disease. All types of distemper cause the body temperature of the dog to rise. The eyes discharge a mucous secretion and the nose runs profusely. Sometimes diarrhea, prolonged and bloody, follows an attack.

Distemper is caused by a virus, the smallest living cell we know, much smaller than a bacterium. There are cures for some types of distemper but there is a preventative that is much safer and less costly! If you value your dog's life, immunize him against distemper by a series of injections. Consult your vet as soon as you have purchased your puppy.

The simplest and most easily cured form of distemper is the skin type. It manifests itself by the appearance of an abundance of postules on the body of the dog.

Nervous distemper results in severe fits and convulsions. Paralysis and death usually follow. This form of distemper is usually a secondary infection to one of the other forms of distemper. Most veterinarians will request permission to destroy your dog once paralysis sets in. Even those few dogs that may survive the paralysis are left with chorea, a palsied condition, which makes their muscles so weak that they fall off their feet from time to time.

Respiratory and intestinal distemper are other forms of distemper. The respiratory form affects the nasal and sinus passages as well as the lungs and bronchi. The intestinal form affects the alimentary tract. Though these may not be fatal if they are treated with miracle drugs (streptomycin, penicillin, etc.), they are usually followed by nervous distemper.

## RABIES

Rabies is the most fatal disease to which a dog may fall victim. It is incurable when it reaches a certain stage and is highly contagious when a dog or person is bitten by an infected animal. But, it is possible to immunize your dog against rabies. Consult your local veterinarian for advice on the type of injections he recommends. There are two known types of rabies: furious and dumb. The furious rabies manifests itself very dramatically. The dog goes wild, running in all directions and biting anything and everything in its path. A rabid dog has even been known to savagely attack the tires on an automobile, tearing his mouth and losing his teeth in the process. After this fit the infected dog usually convulses and dies.

The dumb rabies affects the infected animal in a very different manner. This type of rabid dog cowers in the corner and appears to be just down-hearted and "blue." Finally the dog will die. Sometimes a dog infected with dumb rabies might snap at the person who approaches him.

Rabies is as fatal to man and some other animals as it is to dogs. The only time diagnosis can be obtained with certainty is after the animal has been killed and the brain examined by a trained pathologist. If you suspect your dog or any other animal of having rabies, do not destroy him. He must be kept under observation and studied. Call your doctor, veterinarian or local health authority if you suspect a rabies case.

If you are ever bitten by any dog, report it immediately. Rabies can be cured by a very complicated and uncomfortable procedure, provided the disease has not reached beyond a certain point. Have the dog placed under observation to ascertain whether he is rabid or not. Remember: Rabies is fatal if unchecked. Play it safe and report every dog bite.

## FITS

Dogs occasionally have fits or convulsions which in a few hours disappear and seem to leave the dog none the worse. This type of disorder may be the result of any one of many possible disorders. Dogs have been known to have fits because of rabies, epilepsy, distemper, worms, overheating, indigestion, a foreign object stuck somewhere in the digestive tract, fright or nervousness. Frequent fits over an extended period indicate some basically serious disease. Place the dog in a cool, safe, dark room and call your veterinarian.

## HOW TO WEIGH YOUR DOG

The fluctuation in your dog's weight is important as a checkpoint in his health. Worms, external parasites, faulty diet and other disorders manifest themselves by affecting his general health. By checking your dog's weight periodically you can foresee serious consequences of a long unattended ailment.

The easiest method of weighing your dog is to hold him in your arms and step on the scale. After you have noted the combined weight of yourself and your dog, weigh yourself alone. The difference between the two weights is the weight of your dog.

## YOUR VETERINARIAN

Your local vet is your best friend. You should consult him when you buy your dog. List his telephone number in your telephone book in case of emergency. Consult him for any major ailment that may affect your cocker spaniel.

Remember this: *It is better to be safe than sorry!*

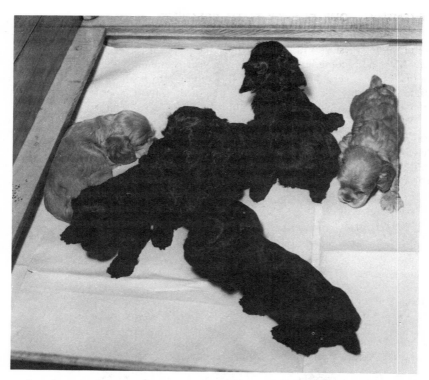

In a few weeks these pups will be ready for new homes. When choosing a puppy, check first to see that it is a healthy one and has no discharge from its eyes or ears, nor a runny nose. (Photo Louise Van de Meid)

# 6. Breeding Your Cocker Spaniel

Owning a dog and not breeding her is like owning a boat and not going fishing.

Pure-bred dogs have been developed only because people had the foresight and intelligence to breed their pets. This has promoted and intensified those qualities for which the breed is noted. Without this type of sensible breeding many of the popular breeds would never have come into existence.

You, as a pet owner, are faced with several problems when you own a female of the breed. You can either breed her once in a while and enjoy the puppies (and the extra income they will bring you when you sell them), or you can prevent her from breeding. Let's take a look at each possibility.

## PREVENTING YOUR COCKER FROM BREEDING

If you want to prevent your female from breeding, you must consider several things. First you must understand the physical aspect of the breeding cycle. Most dogs come into "heat" twice a year, some only once every 8 or 9 months, others every 4 or 5 months. By coming into heat we mean that the female is not only receptive to a male dog in the physical sense, but that if she mates, in all probability she will ultimately have her puppies.

When a female comes into heat, her external sexual organs swell into very large size and a slight discharge of blood and mucus will be noticed. Once the discharge stops, or at least slows down quite a bit, the female will be receptive to a male for mating. The time involved is usually about one week for a swelling of the vulva, one week for the course of the discharge, and a final week when the vulva starts to shrink again.

The best time to breed the dog is as soon as the discharge stops. Most breeders prefer to breed on the first and third days after the stop of the discharge. They feel that this double fertilization insures complete coverage.

If you do not want your female dog to breed, then you must keep her penned up, away from all breeds of dogs, during this 3-week period.

Cocker Spaniels usually make concerned and attentive mothers.

Some fanciers purchase a chemical preparation which is supposed to be very offensive to the male dog. By applying this to your female in heat, you will keep the males at a distance. This is not a completely safe method, though it is advisable to use the chemical anyway in case your dog should escape while she is in heat. (When escaping they usually try to get to male company.)

A special harness, which not only absorbs the discharge but in a mechanical way protects the female against a male, is available too. However, the only *sure* means is to pen in the female securely so she cannot get out and another dog cannot get in.

"Spaying" is the term applied to an operation in which the veterinarian removes the female dog's ovaries. Once your female has been spayed she can never have puppies. Oftentimes a spayed female will grow plump and lazy unless she is exercised frequently.

Most dog clubs will not allow a spayed female to be entered into competition.

## SELECTING A MATE FOR YOUR DOG

If you intend to breed your dog, keep this in mind: It is just as easy to raise perfect puppies as poor ones. If you will devote a little forethought to this and spend a few extra dollars in the beginning, you will be paid off handsomely later on.

When you buy your dog is the time to decide whether or not to breed her. At that time you should inquire from the breeder or shop from whom you purchase, where a good sire can be obtained. If you have a certain color variety in mind, ask for that color dog (though the genetics of dogs is a complicated subject, and you might sometimes be very surprised). Try to get a good sire who has, in his pedigree, a good common relative to your own dog. Mating dogs that are too closely related may be a bit dangerous, genetically, though usually every breed originates from a single pair.

After you have selected the sire, make arrangements when the female goes into heat to breed her. Call the owner of the sire as soon as your dog has the discharge and make an appointment for the following week. Breed your dog once or twice within that period, following cessation of the discharge.

In the contract between the owner of the sire and yourself stipulate, if possible, that you would like to include return service in the fee. This means that if your female does not get pregnant from the first breeding that you will get a free service during the next reproductive cycle. Usually the breeder will want a small extra fee for this service. Whatever you do make all arrangements in writing. Sometimes you might forget important details and a lot of trouble may be the result.

## THE FEMALE IN WHELP

The gestation period for most dogs in the temperate zone (United States, Canada, England, Australia, etc.) is 63 days. This may vary a day or so but it is a fairly accurate gauge. If your dog does not have her puppies within 65 days, consult your vet. Some dogs may need assistance in having their puppies but they usually can do the job without any help.

You will notice, as your female begins to fill in, that her appetite will increase until she must be fed twice a day instead of once a day. Give her as much as she wants to eat and allow her to exercise as much as usual during the first four or five weeks. After this period give her plenty of walking exercise but try to keep her from jumping about too much.

During the last weeks it is very helpful if you have a whelping box prepared. This can be a cardboard or wooden box high enough so the female can comfortably be stretched out and stand without hitting her head (if it has a roof). The idea is to make it high enough to keep the puppies from climbing out, but low enough for the mother dog to enter and leave without hurting herself.

Place plenty of clean papers flat on the bottom and accustom your female to it a week or so before she is to whelp. Keep the whelping box clean at all times.

When the puppies come, give the female all she wants to eat and drink. Give her milk and plenty of vitamins and minerals. It is especially important to include these supplements in the whelping diet.

## WHELPING

As with all animals, whelping is a natural process and does not, under normal circumstances, require the assistance of a veterinarian.

When your female dog goes into labor. keep your eye on her. She will probably whimper now and then, but that is only natural and should not cause any alarm. If she has been in labor for seven or eight hours and she still has not delivered her first puppy, or after several hours she has not delivered her second, then you should call in your veterinarian immediately.

Unless she needs help, do not disturb her. Usually she will make certain that her puppies are kept warm; she'll sleep with them and not on them. When all the puppies have been delivered, sponge the puppies' navels with cotton soaked in rubbing alcohol. The mother dog will usually eat the afterbirth, and you should allow her to do that, because it contains special hormones which start off certain bodily processes (milk production, etc.).

Do not handle the puppies the first few days and definitely do not allow strangers (human or animal) to excite the mother dog. Keep the mother and her litter as warm and comfortable as possible. Keep the whelping box clean and change it daily with a minimum amount of disturbance.

Once the puppies' eyes open (about ten days after birth), you can begin to handle them more and more. Do not place them in direct sunlight yet as their eyes are very sensitive to strong light for a few days after they first open.

After the puppies are 3 weeks old, they will become playful and wander about. This is the time to allow them more freedom and to begin their toilet training. Even month-old puppies will not dirty their own sleeping quarters, so place a little bit of paper outside the whelping box and by the time the puppies are old enough to sell (about 6 weeks . . . some even at 5 weeks) they will be paper-broken.

## WEANING THE PUPPIES

Weaning your puppies is a slow and, at times, exasperating process. Wean the puppies gradually so neither the mother dog nor the puppies are upset by any sudden changes. Inspect the dam's breasts every day to ascertain whether her milk is accumulating too fast and is in danger of caking. If her breasts get hard you may have to milk off the surplus by hand and rub her breasts with warm camphorated oil.

Feed the puppies on cereal or fine dog food mixed with warm milk and softened to a semi-liquid consistency. Allow the puppies all they can eat in 20 minutes four times a day. Try to arrange a feeding schedule that you can follow every day, say, at 8 A.M., noon, 4 P.M. and 8 P.M. Feed them only at this time and let them take their snacks betwen meals from their mother.

As the puppies' teeth begin to grow, the dam will try to speed up the weaning process herself because the puppies will hurt her when they bite her breasts, so cooperate and have enough nourishment available for her puppies.

In the actual weaning process start like this: After the puppies are 3 weeks old, feed the dam in a very large shallow dish. The puppies will see her eating and the bowl will be shallow enough so they stick their little heads in for a bite. If a puppy doesn't feed, take him individually to the pan while the dam is feeding there and shove his mouth into it so he will get a taste of the luke warm mixture of milk and very fine dog food or cereal and vitamins.

If the puppies do not start eating that meal, try it again at the next mealtime. Keep doing this until they are eating a little each meal. Keep this up for a week until the puppies are 4 weeks old, then feed them away from the dam 3 times daily. Gradually give their mother more and more free time away from them. Finally after 6 weeks they should be able to eat by themselves.

Some puppies eat like horses! This is okay provided they do not eat their brothers' food. Make sure that each puppy has his share of the meal even if it means feeding one or two of them separately on occasion.

## DOCKING THE COCKER PUPPIES' TAILS

It is general practice to dock the tails of all cocker spaniels. Call in your vet within 72 hours after the puppies are born and have him do the job for you. It is best to have the cocker's tail docked when he is 3 days old.

Make sure that the vet knows the exact length to dock and that he leaves you instructions on what to do after the operation. Docking the tails at this age is painless.